It's The Context

Sherna Spencer

It's The Context Copyright © 2017, by Sherna G. Spencer. All rights reserved.
Except as permitted under the U.S. Copyright Act of 1976, no part of this publication may be reproduced, distributed, or transmitted in any form or by any means, or stored in a database or retrieval system, without the prior written permission of the publisher.

Published by JALOUSIE
An imprint of SGS Publishing, LLC
4500 W. Oakland Park Boulevard, Ste 103
Fort Lauderdale, FL 33313
www.lookitsthebook.com
Talk@lookitsthebook.com

Cover design: Sunita Spencer-Archer and John Vincent Palozzi

It's The Context is a work of fiction. Names, characters, places, and incidents are the product of the author's imagination or are used fictionally. Any resemblance to actual events, locales, or persons, living or dead, is coincidental.

Publisher's Cataloging-in-Publication data

Spencer, Sherna G
    It's The Context: 42 collected poems, 2016-2017/Sherna Spencer
        p.cm
        Includes index
        ISBN 978-0-9787613-9-4
        1. Caribbean. 2. Poetry. Women writers.
        3. Inspirational-Women.
        4. Humor –Women. 5.Title-

    Library of Congress Control number: 2017910889
    First Edition: August 2017   SCANNABLE

    Printed in the United States of America

    Attention Corporations, Universities, Colleges and Professional Organizations.
    Quantity Discounts are available on bulk purchases of this book for educational, gift purposes, or as premiums for increasing magazine subscriptions or renewals.
    Special books or book excerpts can also be created to fit specific needs. For Information, please contact SGS Publishing, 4500 W. Oakland Park Boulevard, Suite 103
    Fort Lauderdale, FL 33313: 954-714-8123.

Context is in your pores
it's in the atmosphere and in the
people around you

Context happens
Contextually

Context is when
I, we, he, she, they or you
caused it

I pray for understanding, patience,
determination and health
to handle my context

Dedication

To my aunt Patsy,
a survivor who has turned
the **con** into the **pro**

Acknowledgements

The Author wishes to express
her gratitude to her editor,
John Vincent Palozzi

TABLE OF CONTENTS

Live
All TOLD	17
Context	18
It Will Find You	20
Living Lively	21

Rising at Sunset
All I Have	25
Chalk Dust	27
Here to There	28
Leaving Time	29
Oh Jah Jah	30
Robber Bands	35
See Me	37
Summer Contentment	39
The Private	40
Who Am I	41

Social Commentary
American Pie	47
Definitions	49
Drones	54
Free Will	56
Keep Your Clothes On	57
Move	59
New Rules and Tools	60

Outsider	61
PAN AM747	62
Status Quo	64
The Ceiling	65
Trains	67

Leaning In

He Touched Me	71
I See You	73
I Wonder	74
I'm IN	75
Inside	76
Matter Matters	77
Part and Parcel, We	78
Today Is Different	80

First Impressions

72 Degrees in Miami	85
Answers Evading Questions	87
Bullish	89
Culture Shock, Florida	90
Dressed Up For An Outing	91
Dressed Up For An Outing— Response	92
Getting 'Round Town, Island Style	93
Impression	95
Lover Boy	96
Take Me To The Ball	97

Table Of Contents Story
TOCstory™

All and truth be Told, Living Lively is Defining Who Am I, Moving away from the Status Quo, exercising my Free Will. I made the decision not hoping that It Will Find me; I decided that Today is Different, it's Leaving Time, time to be Bullish like an Outsider, taking the Matter in my own hands, breaking through the glass Ceiling, after He Touched Me. It was the Context they said, but for me, Culture Shock. Today it is 72 Degrees in Miami, not a beach day, so we decided to Keep our Clothes On and still make an Impression. We took the Train, to Get Around the Town and there he was Lover Boy, all Dressed UP for an Outing. Now I don't have to Wonder why his Answers Evaded my Questions. It's New Rules and Tools, Jah Jah, See Me, I'm In; all of us, all Part and Parcel We, are flying from Here to There, tomorrow on The Private 747, enjoying American Pie, Inside. All I will Have in my hand luggage, is my Dress for the Ball in the evening, the Chalk dust — rose colored one, where my band, the Drones, will be honored. We will be Contented this summer, no one will Rob our band of this honor.

ALL Told

Attitude (exhibiting good)
Latitude (having compassion/consideration)
Longitude (thinking long term)

A life well lived, is TOLD by ALL of these

It's the Context

Context

Context is the
> subtext
> back story
> man behind the mask
> reason
> *rasison d'etre*
> grey area
> circumstance that altered the case
> predicate of the subject
> Juliet that caused the Romeo
> straw that broke the camel's back
> lynchpin
> devil in the details
> justification
> domino effect
> perfect storm of events
> nuance that caused the resistance

Context sometimes
breathes fire
or explodes a dam

When overflowing, it
shatters the pretext
of common language
it questions the depth of love

Some may define it as complex
but it's not a Rolex

Live

Context wants more than to be seen and heard
by the herd

Context wants a do-over
by the movers

Context wants the shakers
to put weights on
and move the **con** from the **text**
from which time
all shall be
subjects
and not
objects
of the world

It's the Context

It Will Find You

We all want to know
that there is a reason for our being

We search our minds
at times
in quiet solitude

We rise each day
hoping that
as certain as the dawn
we will discover our purpose

It is written
that all men are created equal
on purpose

Keep looking
it will find you

Living Lively

Living is what you do
instinctively
thought
propelled by action
to satisfy
an innate
need

Living lively is taking a stance
to make your footprint
to stamp your mark
on the world today

Do it

The universe
is waiting

Rising at Sunset

All I have

All I have to give you
is what I am
what I was born in
from the womb

Flesh, my safety net
a surround sound stretching head to toe
and bones interlocking
holding my insides in place

All I have to give you
is what I am
inside
in my mind

My thoughts
my feelings
explained by a foreign language
not native to my being

Me, my being
in total nakedness
contains my desire to live
to be
free
to be the
human ingredient that makes this planet
Live

It's the Context

That is all I have to give you
It is the best of me

Our planet lives
from the pure unadulterated energy
that radiates from within us

We are an essential ingredient
in our planet's song

Love

Live

The planet gives
what it receives
from us

Chalk Dust

Specks of violet dust
fly off the slate in all directions till its black background is
laid bare

With each speck a
wrench of unforgotten pain is
tempered

I endured them — each and every
screech and poke of the chalk
searing lines of violet across my blackboard

The wounds laid there
bare
for decades

It's the Context

Here to Here

Are we there yet?

Living between the raindrops
every day coming closer
but not quite there
between bedlam and victory
root beer and cognac

Humming in the car to the cued-up radio song
on my way to a mingle
running in late
missing the full song
still single

Are we there yet?

My soul perpetually seeking
for the honey cluster
it which to satiate itself
awoke to a new sunrise

Wide, bold multi colored lines
indicated where to go

My senses reacted in harmony upon arrival
and he is there
waiting in the
rainbow

Leaving Time

What do you take from a smile
and an exchange of thoughts that lingers
long after the words are spoken
. . . we could get married and run away to Ecuador

The earth stopped
then started again

It released a strong wind
that made music

It danced
and whistled its way through the tall grass
straight out to the shore
where it whipped the waters high
then smashed down
shivering
burrowing into the deep unknown

. . . Ecuador, what's in Ecuador?

It's the Context

Oh Jah Jah

(The summer and fall of my discontent: Eulogy for the Caribbean-American planters*)

I feel almost inconsolable. I have Bob Marley in my mind, the rhythmic beat and his voice repeatedly remarking "*oh Jah Jah, oh Jah Jah, oh Jah Jah Jah, oh Jah Jah Jah — yeah yeah….*" "Goodness gracious Lord have mercy…" What was he thinking, what made him write those words — was he so much in love that he was wondering why Jah had filled him with so much happiness? Maybe he had just had a revelation about life or his purpose here and it made him more reverend, more in awe? That song had to have been inspired by a new revelation. What was it Bob?

I am searching for that revelation and a bit of consolation: What will be my song?

The lions and lionesses are going, leaving us, leaving forever, to return to their maker. Their tracks, their paw prints are indelibly left on my psyche, pressed into my soul's memory banks. At some point, they will become a distant memory, like the typewriter or the mortar (*mata*), something once indispensable, now replaced by another some(one)thing that is more in need?

Who will knead the flour that made those unforgettable dumplings that accompanied the more unforgettable *ackee* and salt fish? Ah, I feel that I have not yet learnt enough, I have not yet mastered mackerel rundown, the rice and peas . . . "don't go!"

In my mind's eye I see fingers adeptly put a quick fix to the tear in the uniform, then perfected it with an iron crease. The tender palm lifting our chins to examine face and hair, before turning us around for a final inspection, sometimes adding a dab of lotion to an elbow or hair oil — to lay down a stubborn curl before shooing us out the door for our school day with our bag, pencil and lunch in tow.

~

When a friend said to me that he was looking for a real trench woman as a life mate, I instinctively knew he meant her — the matter of fact, got any job done calmly; though once in a great while, with a lot less calm! Confident, loving, fun. That *trenchie* made her mark on him (us), grooming us with a multitude of prompts: humor, God, Miss Lou, The Queen, "always rise to the occasion" and the dreaded "jus wait till yuh father come."

Who will make my tie-a-leaf.?

I feel empty, there is so much I want to take from them, so much of them that is me. I do not know what to do, think or say. I see the children who will never understand how I feel — they can only feel what they feel, their experience with them is not mine.

The decades unfold as I look into their faces; hers smiling, wearing the crinoline and pressed cotton dresses, hair pressed with hot combs, curlers; women mothering and fathering, putting us first, putting themselves in us, expecting us to do more, to represent them and make them proud.

His face, appears the lion, who also was a philosopher, explaining why things are the way they are and declare what was and still is important to our lives, *Ska* or the *Skatalites* or the *Tamlins*; the use for the herbs, baking soda, other "bush" medicines; Maker of hot peanuts, sky juice, hotter shrimps from wicker baskets.

His smooth face, ah, he was the stoic, the buck stops here decider, the walk or drive out on Sunday for ice cream or the walk next door or down the road — maybe for a game of dominoes or *ludi*, he had the hands that brought the sweets and treats, changed the tire, put the potato slips and peas in the earth. He was the cutter of the coconut, the crab catcher, the record spinner, the once in a while mannish water chef.

The man, the Man's man, the confidence of being in charge of your destiny which was the first to go after migrating...now that you are in another Man's country; leaving was not an option for most and some left, others stayed reluctantly, some accepted the interruption, the pause, their potential suspended in a foreign clime where everyday bruises chipped away at the soul.

Who heard the sigh in the dark, *oh Jah Jah Jah, oh Jah Jah Jah, oh Jah Jah Jah* . . . . Those words said there is no consolation, this place is against the soul. . . .

Jah Jah . . . Thy kingdom come on earth, thy will be done on earth.

It's the Context

Who will take charge of the job they started? I realize now that they were not meant to finish it. Someone must come and make an improvement, make their own contribution. Oh *Jah Jah*, Oh *Jah Jah*. They made us who we are — she held the keys to our hearts and lives or he held the door, directing and watching us fly.

We will meet them again. Our souls will sit and reminisce.

Oh, Jah, Jah, who art in heaven, hallowed be thy name, thy kingdom come on earth, thy will be done on earth. Hallowed be thy name.

*the mavericks, first comers to America

Robber Bands

Our bodies contain rubber bands.
They're time robbers.
Pushing and pulling
they extend and retract
instantaneously,
with spontaneity
when youth
propels.
just in time

Otherwise they are uncaring louts.
Even when you shout.
They meander
from here to there
slowly,
frustrating
our commands
and wishes.
taking their own sweet time

They are robber bands.
Laying in wait.
They live within us
attempting to steal
our lives,
trying to slow us down
like stubborn
stiff necked
oppositionists

It's the Context

Be the party in power.
Rout them out.
Fight them to the ground
and stuff them till they're stout
with memories,
moments
actions and
activities
benefiting our health and wealth

Follow my lead.
They'll yield.
We'll lick them on the field
If we practice every day
we'll have our way
and sing **our** tune
to the robber
and their
band.

See ME

See my pores
lying flat
a lazy worker
the blocker
fighting the rain, wind and sun
with
indolent
insolence

See my eyes
though constantly wet
runs only when the heart decrees

The balls stand
on purpose
and swing side to side
while the eyelid is on guard
blink open
blink shut
without a care for
my agreement or opposition
protecting the mystery
of the inner me

See my nails
almost translucent
after being submerged in liquid
— so soft I can tear them with my fingers

Give them some air time

and they harden their position
without being pressed into doing so

See my hair
that my hairdresser loves on her less busy days

Its roots in tight formation
can be carefully coiffed or left to run wild
I decide

My gene pool won the battle in the womb
against the "thin is in"
declaring "thick it is"

See me translucent
blood, cells, bone
designed by
a mind
and
a hand
formidable in its
decision to
produce
perfection
inside out

Summer Contentment

It is summer.
I am content
a sun-filled seed
not choked out by the weeds

I am emerging
from a spring
planting
which took centuries
from design to completion
of an outer shell of hair, skin and nails
guarding the inner engine
organs, blood, arteries and capillaries.
my fighting spirit

My seed was planted
in the most nourishing
productive soil,
then fertilized
by the maker.
I emerge
I emerge
I emerge
victorious

It's the Context

The Private

There is a me
that you can't see

I need it to be

I need it to be undercover
I need it to be inside
I need it to be silent
I need it to be the director
I need it to be my champion
I need it to be the thinker
I need it to be the stopper
I need it to be the look before you leap
I need it to be the flash of insight that makes me do
      the things that I do

I need it

It allows me
to
be
the
me
that
you
see

Am I who I am
(Who am I)

Am I the
taste buds that went to Italy
and returned
still entirely ingrained
with blisters from my curry fixation?

Am I the
sightless energy beams
that occupy the cells
that moves at my mind's beck and call

Lift hand
Open palms
Close fingers to hold the pen
put it on the paper
form a letter

Or did my hand, palm and finger decide to move
and then dragged my mind along?

Did it beat my will into submission...
this first
then whatever you want to do later...

Who decided what I want to or must do?

Am I the
darkness, the void that fills my face

It's the Context

when I close my eyes?

Is it always waiting for permission to tell my body to be still
when I want to listen to the humming
the music
the breath
the blood, food and oxygen
taking turns
fine tuning my body?

Am I the
voice, a bit of the Jamaica countryside still stuck in America?

Some say it is commanding

<u>Ira</u> said it is unique, one of a kind

I thought it rather ordinary, but he wants encores

I'll just have to move in, he declares boldly

Will it sound to him the same at midnight 3am or 7am?

Does it do anything to my insides?

Can I change its everyday pitch or intonation?

What if I move to a different location or
choose another vocation?

Am I the
thought that chases in fleeting movements across my face
that is reflected on my cheeks and lips?

Perhaps I am found in the tiny smirk which emerged
triumphant
when I tried to hide the bubble of mirth that made my
chest tremble

Yes and maybe I am the me that makes me keep my spine
straightened
pulling up my legs
stiff upper lip and go for the gold
or maybe I am my step that bounces my hips (keep going
till you get it, my insides remind me)?

Am I the
way my bones connect on their joints
click, click, click, click, click, click
like dominoes
when everything comes together and you win
all six games back to back

Yeah 6 love

It's the Context

Give me love 6 times
anytime

I came into and
will leave my body, the cage that holds me in this cosmos

When I go, I will release my signature perfume
that will be bouncing
gliding and
riding the winds in the atmosphere
forever

I am me

Social Commentary

Social Commentary

American Pie

America is mom and apple pie
wheat bread and Rye

America is a beef burrito
pieces of prosciutto
black beans and
soup du jour
in under half an hour

America is potato pancakes
jasmine rice and
doubles. Jerk chicken
boiled dumplings
caviar and
white chardonnay

America is Louis Armstrong
Alexander Hamilton
Bette Midler
the rolling stones
Babe Ruth
Dr. Ruth (Westheimer)
Deeprak Chopra, Oprah
Jimmy Carter
the Muppets
the Chipmunks
Julie Andrews
John Wayne

It's the Context

America is the plantation
the zero lot line

Stop there
our children need space
to race

America drives
a pink Cadillac

She rocks with Camaro

She tours in a Ford
or even nicer
in a Chrysler

Even a dolt
could figure it out

America is

America was

America will be
you and me

WE

Definitions

If you look closely at my left arm
you will see a scar from the injection for measles

So too with my knees; both carry scars and bits of scars
evidencing numerous falls on uneven ground
after climbing on orange and guava trees
and running away from bees

Beneath my left eyebrow is a half-moon reminder
of the first attempts to make my own kite
a revolt against my uncle's refusal
to make me one

Those were minor aches and pains
eclipsed by life's
ups and downs
falls, pitfalls
business and relationship
fits, starts
revelations and reinventions

I can say it
I can talk about it
I can say who I am
the me
that became

ME

It's the Context

Though my language is borrowed
my voice is my own

So don't define me

I come from white marl and red dirt
rich in minerals and nutrients
passed down, generation to generation
so to grow the yam, sweet potato and corn
roasted outside
between the rocks made too from hills
of white marl and red dirt
It is forever buried beneath and in my fingernails
unseen but ready to do battle
for my soul
an indelible reminder of the beginnings from which I came

Don't define me

I come from the lilies
that swam in the rock ponds
that the frogs called home in the rain

My lips and hands tasted
and my nostrils inhaled the fragrance
of the thick mist
that rose visibly

oozing up from the ground
peppered with

dandelions and Spanish needle

Don't define me

I come from feet planted
all ten toes buried six feet
under
part of the stratosphere down below

The feeling of the live earth
penetrated through my body

My umbilical cord is attached there
hidden
deep in their
folds
raw only touched by the maker's hands

Don't define me

I come from the tar
rolled lavishly over and onto the
white marl and red dirt
and the scents steamed into my soul
from the sugar cane
rum
ginger
and the small fires that burned day and night island wide

It's the Context

chugging out curries and stews
from makeshift outside kitchens
and gas and electric stoves in the
mansions in the hills

These scents planted themselves into my esophagus
and declared
they've found their home

So don't define me

I come from crisp attention straight as a saw uniforms
that protected me, guarding my body
with quite countenance
giving my brain full power to
riot
to roam and tabulate, calculate
analyze and memorize
the lesson of the day

There they sat
and still remain
unperturbed
saturating my memory pores

Don't define me

I come, I come from Lilieth and Cassell
I come from Lilybelll and Arthur
I come from the trade winds off the Atlantic Ocean

Social Commentary

the rough seas of the Arctic and Mediterranean

They brought a seed
a seed that became ME

A small part
of that ME
is the ME
that you SEE

So

don't

define

ME

that is for me to do

It's the Context

Drones

On the job in nondescript buildings
Heads down
minding their own business
noncommittal
some nocturnal
conforming nonconformists

Until the clock strikes 5:00

At a local restaurant
I joined the line to order and pay for my food

There were about seven persons ahead of me

The customer being served
was talking with the server
while her order was being packaged

She smiled
then laughed out loud

As her words rolled off her tongue
her accent flipped it and it flew
bouncing on the nearby air pockets

The server laughed too
and the next two persons behind her

I was too far away to hear, but my lips parted
seeking to join in the revelry

In a jaunty stride she turned towards the exit
cradling her food

She continued to chuckle as she walked through the
doorway
spirited
engaging
flamboyant
lively

It's the Context

Free Will

Free will
takes up space

It's when I am
requested to go through the turnstile at the game for the count (body)
scanned for identification (eyelid, fingers)
taken for investigation (liquids)
shaved for security (hair and face)
graphed for a DNA match (skin)
plucked for observation (hair)

Free will
has evaporated into thin air

I need a spare

Keep Your Clothes On

Frustration
trepidation
amazement
anxiety
fear
as you contemplate a TRUMPEXIT

The Brits are taking their pill
but we don't have to wait
for our morning after

Keep your clothes on and your wits about you

Announce it
use a TRUMPET
say
I have a
trumpCARD that I can share

I will deploy it
with your help
my fellow Americans

Let's remain high from the heady DNC love fest

Keep your clothes on and your wits about you

It's the Context

Follow our lead undecideds and independents

Let us be the deciders

Let us play our cards
we can TRIUMPH

We can get over the hump
without a British bump

Exercise your right

In November show your might
don't contemplate taking flight

Just keep your clothes on and your wits about you

MOVE

Children's tools
pencils
rubbers
slates and
skates
hands and feet on the move

In a twinkle of an eye
they are replaced

Move
I mutter
plaintively
softly
wishing
I could diffuse my breath
to another use
to be the engine behind stiff legs

Move
like you used to

I need some
new tools

It's the Context

New Rules and Tools
(for fools?)

Old school teaching
Bring your book, read more and more
Memorize the verses
as there might come a day
when you do not have the book
and you will know the words
They would guide you
through whatever you are facing

New school rules
The book is just too heavy
These days it's about brevity
Come today, I will give you some nuggets
come tomorrow for a bit more
Bringing books says you are a bore
No time to memorize
it's a devise for the wise
trying to bring you down a size

If you come
we'll give you a prize

Outsider

The cornmeal dumpling is
calling me

My toes are itching to
trod on Spanish Needle and Rockstone

My ears are being
pulled to suck in the vibrations from the rain on the zinc of
the chicken coop, as they
stand calm, huddled, taking the beating for acts they did
not commit

My nostrils want to nuzzle nose to nose with familial
brethren and
inhale familiar scents, so my lips and tongue will
carry our recollections forward to the next generation

But something is always lost – the kitchen bitch, *mata*
(mortar) and Bata shoes

It's the Context

PAN AM 747

Free to fly high
free to touch the sky

With a ticket in my given name
I said my goodbyes
to my pet name
to granny
to eating heartily
to walking and running fearlessly
to spontaneity
simplicity,
self-definition
Self

Woooosh across the clouds

Hello new world
where time
where simplicity
where objectivity
where explanations
love
stops for no one

It's one against one

It defines the game, the name
the thoughts
the talk the walk

Social Commentary

All are orchestrated
to fit into a ready-made square
It devours you and
yourself

If you don't mind sharp

The pet name
is left in the cloud
along with a past
hazy
to the
recollection
but longed
for

It's the Context

Status Quo

Status quo
Lo
It stands guard

You get
You give
Something shifts
How far?

The Ceiling

Woman
watch the glass
It sees thee
Climb
Prepare
be
armed
and ready

We have toiled in the fields of commerce
deploying strategies
assembling
dissembling
attempting to upend
the status
quo
NO

We have planted our cause far and near
employing charm
sometimes conspiring
and disarming
*tact*icts
and gazes
in phases
Wasted

A new week
demands a new technique

It's the Context

not a wiki-leak

Let's get on our Trojan horse
Be Greek
and move the mountain
with our pen
Bring friends

Trains

At each stop
new riders arrive
old riders depart

For a time they ride together
sharing moments
the noise from the brakes easing down to stop
its undulating movements change
while tackling the earth's terrain
the maze of corners; hills and valleys
the weather's tempestuousness

The driver adjusts
speeding up or slowing down
seeking to arrive at the predetermined time and
to avoid a catastrophe

The train is always moving toward a destination
its role is to take you to your goal

Both the train and the passenger knows
where it will stop
though neither can guarantee
or say for sure
what will happen
on the way there

**Vibing on "Prince," his life and death

He Touched Me

I sat there
a storm of words swirling
around me

I marveled at myself

I am at peace
calm

A few years ago
while in the same place
I thought
too LOUD, clash of cymbals

Run

I sat there

The bass, the lights
the people
speaking out
speaking of their love
wants
needs
desires
intensely
with intensity

It's the Context

I sat there
a thought slid
to the forefront of my mind
this is HOME

I remained still
consciously
waiting
listening

II

I sat there
and while the storm of voices swirled around me
he took my right hand
and held it

I do now know
how he knew
it needed it to be held
and then he planted his message into my consciousness

He said
believe and find peace
your backup is always here
paving the way

The scriptures say faith is the substance of things hoped
for and the evidence of things not seen

I See You

He told me
stay strong
Nothing can go wrong
you belong
to my throng

Now I'm stepping into me
the me that he made me to be
I was healed from the gritty
now banned
let's go glitzy!
To the Ritz
with Carlton
and children in tow

It's the Context

I Wonder

I wonder if my off spring 5,000 years from now
will wonder what I was like

Will someone say
5,000 years ago there was someone related to me
what was she like
what language did she speak
Where or how did she live
What did she eat
What did she wear
What did she fear?

I wonder if 5000 years from now the grass will be green

Will children still play "Simon says?"

Which transgressions will rue the day

Will we be swimming to get around

How will we sound

Will visiting be old-style rudimentary
along with talking and touching

Maybe they will all be gone with the wind
extinct
like faux pauxs, and mules

I am also left to ponder the
reason for that flash of thunder

I'm IN

I'm
IN
THE most significant
Role of a lifetime
Living
not to be
insignificant

Inside

Inside there is an
inner sense —
in a sense

This inner sense
is an inner feeling
of who you are
the real you
the inner person
the insider
the know all
the all-knowing —
in a sense

We are all carrying
something
something we cannot name
it's just within but still
slightly
out of out of reach
it's
something from whence we came
it's something
that we are always
seeking to know

Matter Matters

Matter takes up space
Between the ears
Raises our fears

Matter weighs
on our souls
the scales bow

Matter Is corrosive
like sand
In the wrong hand

Matter mostly matters a lot
cannot be left stirring
In the pot

Matter is good
better
 try it
inquire
Sit or walk with it
Look see
feel
taste
smell it's essential
Oil

Matter is better than the rest
It is best
in a group
listening.

Part and Parcel, We

The heavens declare its glory
The earth declares its glory
Our bodies declare its glory
Our brains follow suit

The blueprint
The master plan
The planner
and designer
conceived and
made us
from the simplest seed
to the largest intellectual species
perfect indeed

Each one conceived
to its own purpose
unique

Each designed
to be an interlocking node
independent
but
interdependent

Anything we can
conceive
is shackled and bound
by the same blueprint
our DNA is stamped

Leaning In

to design by template
upon the understanding
that
the whole is stronger
than the individual
part

It's the Context

Today is Different

What a difference a day makes
Today
Not yesterday
Not the day before yesterday
Not last Monday
Not two weeks ago
Not last year
Not your last birthday
Not your last anniversary
Not the last time you thought to do
whatever you did not do

What a difference a day makes
Today
it's 24 hours
6 are gone before you awaken
cherish the second thought that reminds you
of something you almost forgot
cherish that instinct
it guides you
cherish the way you talk
cherish the way you smile
cherish the way you walk
cherish the way you feel as you slide yourself into your clothes
like the hug of a
form fitted button down shirt

What a difference a day makes
Today
Hold the strands of the air around you
organize them
whispers of love and motivation
here
Whispers of negativity
there
behind me
Move with a purpose
eyes wide open
striding
gliding
towards the stars
where your future lies
Today is the day to cherish
Cherish life

72 Degrees In Miami

Four walls vibrate a permanent hummm...........
tearing into my skin's outer layer
kneading into
the fat beneath

My cells
riot
confused
as their natural tendency to
rush to an affected area's aid is
stilled by the sightless, odorless
surround sound that
pushes out insistently
covertly
the frigid, corrosive air

My lips push out short pants of air
they
hung nearby
awaiting instructions

My head moves side to side
rejecting
the sound that
drones on and on
like a car engine
idling with nowhere to go
It's movements say NO
rejecting

It's the Context

grey pockets of air
hovering and circling
the form shrouded in blue and white bedding

Dots fashioned of blue, white and yellow thread
sit on white horizontal lines that weaved into the thin see-through veil
which once cascaded down
adding a designer look to the twin bed it graced

My Fingers and hands
gripped its folds tight around my head and body

I bunched the fabric in front of my stomach

Thick socks hugged my feet and toes
preventing them from being
bitten by the tile's rising frost

Stop

It's killing me

Stop

I need to breathe

Answers Evading Questions

The crows might be able to tell us
they have been around for hundreds of years
flying, watching from above the fray

Did fish every fly
what about the animals
did birds walk
who was the first to talk
was it the chicken then the egg
or vice versa
where are we coming from and
where are we going
and why?

Maybe we should look inside the waters
the whale
or
the sharks
may have the answer

They have existed for thousands of years
guarding their home
from oxygen-breathing intruders

They know
how to keep secrets

Yes, those stoic creatures
gliding quietly
journeying

It's the Context

to and from destinations
to which we are not privy
and not invited to join

I bet they'll know

They've probably stored it
in some obvious
but seemingly unlikely place

I wonder what it takes
to bribe them
into giving it up?

Bullish

Yes you can brag
I'm
Blooming
a
bride
Beaming
bold
bodacious
bountiful

I'm broad
from Bonai to Broadway
and
most of all
bullish on you
teddy bear

It's the Context

Culture Shock, Florida

I started mulling
after I was seeing
people
spending their down time
milling around outside
chilling and
grilling

Others were doing
an inside hideout
Giving the a/c its due
staying in touch with the cable
giving the insects
their day
— time

Can you connect these dots?

The heat pleasers
and the cool creatures

Humanity at the crossroads
both seeking comfort
in their space
in their place

In their carved-out time
they choose how to spend their dime
living under the sun
together but apart

Dressed Up For An Outing

My dress needs an outing
the closet is too conforming

Your tux will be its partner
redux
with throwback necktie
and tails

If conversation sparks
and it lasts
beyond the weather and jester
let's do it again
only grander

Plain is not my name

I'll roll out the silk and satin
baubles and beads
a bustier form-fitted
that would befit
a queen

"Phew," sighs the racks in my closet
"I finally get a break
from the oppressive
and constant weight."

Let's do it
Do
it's up to you

It's the Context

Dressed Up for An Outing – Response

The tux is ready
I ditched the hat
although I might just sport a tam
and mix up the glam

One perfect flower
not a shower
will accompany
your dress

It will be blooming
peak perfection
together they will
get a mention

You will have my 100%
attention and care
all deeds
to suit your needs

Let's start with tux and dress
our spirits
will do the rest

Getting 'Round Town, Island Style

When I was growing up, in Jamaica, we had a term for describing people who were forced to be uncomfortably close to each other. We said "they are as close as sardines in a can." Just imagine the three or four fishes packed in the flat square can, side by side, surrounded by olive oil or water. The liquid provides the lubricant that keeps them together; not too close that they break, just enough for the travel to you.

We used to say the same thing about people in the busses, those tall ones, with their dull red and white paint and wheels the size of a small child. You had to be thankful if you found a bucket seat — sorry for you if you were on a long seat or if you were standing. Keep in mind that their precious cargo was not just within their metal confines. If you looked on top, you would see caged and colorful boxes and bags filled with things belonging to the riders including live animals and other things ready for the pot. Still, the horn was the attention-getter, announcing the busses' presence as they approached corners or to provide a reminder that it was on the move.

No one ever told us we needed to expand our vocabulary. We said the same thing about people in the minibuses and taxicabs — sardines. The people who use these modes of transportation don't ask why, there's no why, it's simply the only way to get around. Murmurs and complaints would surface, not when the minibus or taxi driver says "small up

It's the Context

yuh self," as he stops to pick up another passenger. For the music beats your chest, thumping, preventing conversation. That music is a salve, almost an antibiotic, a way to take your focus away from your discomfort and your embarrassment that your body is as close to a stranger as it is when you are your most intimate.

The drivers do not discriminate you see. Men, women and children perch on each other's bodies, trying not to deliver their full weight on the riders on both sides of them, sometimes while balancing a youngster on their lap. This is a lesson for the weight loss crowd. "Squinge up" he calls out. You pull in your stomach, thighs and anywhere else you can think of to tighten, to compress; the air you breathe is the only lubricant. You turn so you are sitting almost sideways.

The murmurs only start and the faces turn away from those who do not yet know the words Allspice or Ban. Suggestions are provided by the drivers. Some have even raised the bar (your secret is out Victoria).

Yes, the scents go with the sentiments, the latter, a necessary, rather (un)luxurious (albeit interesting) way of traveling around town and sometimes a little farther afield.

The driver, sitting on a piece of wood that is his seat cover, sums everything up tidily
" Yuh not supposed fi too comfortable when yuh a drive."

Impression

I
am
pressing
on
in
the
face
of
in
spite
of
in
the
name
of
Justice
e
s
u
s

It's the Context

Lover Boy

He glanced to his right
looking at his partner
He laughed loudly
Hea Hea

The guffah rocked his upper body
forward and backward
it undulated slowly
like a hammock pushed
but weighted down by an adult body

His cheeks
sprinkled with orange and brown dots
parted upward
pushing his lips apart
showing teeth connected precisely at the gum line
all intact
Large
poster board white
they filled his face
His smile reflected in his eyes; two lighted pools of
brilliance
diamond eyes I called them

As I watched
his hands gripped his partner's momentarily
and they walked past

Take Me To The Ball

Take me to the ball
my dress is ready
the corset which forms a firm
curve-flattering template
stamped particularly for my shape
sits attentively beneath the fabric folds

From bust to toe
it drapes and flairs
reminiscent of the airs
of a bygone time

Take me to the ball
my neck is bedecked with
rhinestones
like the sun
a round globe
anchoring gems
dotting every space
of its circumference
riveting
as far as the eye can see

Take me to the ball
my face is smooth
sponged on bronze powder
the highlights in my hair
radiates
on my
sun dipped skin

It's the Context

Its show time
tonight

Tell me tomorrow your sorrow

Today is for showing
tomorrow is for telling

Other Books By The Author

Musing Aloud, Allowed

Three Echoes Dancing

available on Amazon and Barnes & Noble

About the Author

Sherna Spencer's roots spring from the Island of Jamaica. Her love of books and language began there in a Parish library in Manchester. After moving to the U.S, she attended Le Moyne College in upstate New York. There, she obtained a Bachelors degree, with dual majors in English and Spanish. She continued her studies in Italy and thereafter completed her law degree at the University of Miami School of Law. She is currently an attorney in Fort Lauderdale, Florida where she was the host of a radio program about immigration and nationality law, for 9 years.

www.ingramcontent.com/pod-product-compliance
Lightning Source LLC
Chambersburg PA
CBHW050602300426
44112CB00013B/2039